FREEDOM FIGHTERS FROM UNDIVIDED GOALPARA DISTRICT OF ASSAM

RITURAJ BASUMATARY

Copyright © Rituraj Basumatary
All Rights Reserved.

This book has been published with all efforts taken to make the material error-free after the consent of the author. However, the author and the publisher do not assume and hereby disclaim any liability to any party for any loss, damage, or disruption caused by errors or omissions, whether such errors or omissions result from negligence, accident, or any other cause.

While every effort has been made to avoid any mistake or omission, this publication is being sold on the condition and understanding that neither the author nor the publishers or printers would be liable in any manner to any person by reason of any mistake or omission in this publication or for any action taken or omitted to be taken or advice rendered or accepted on the basis of this work. For any defect in printing or binding the publishers will be liable only to replace the defective copy by another copy of this work then available.

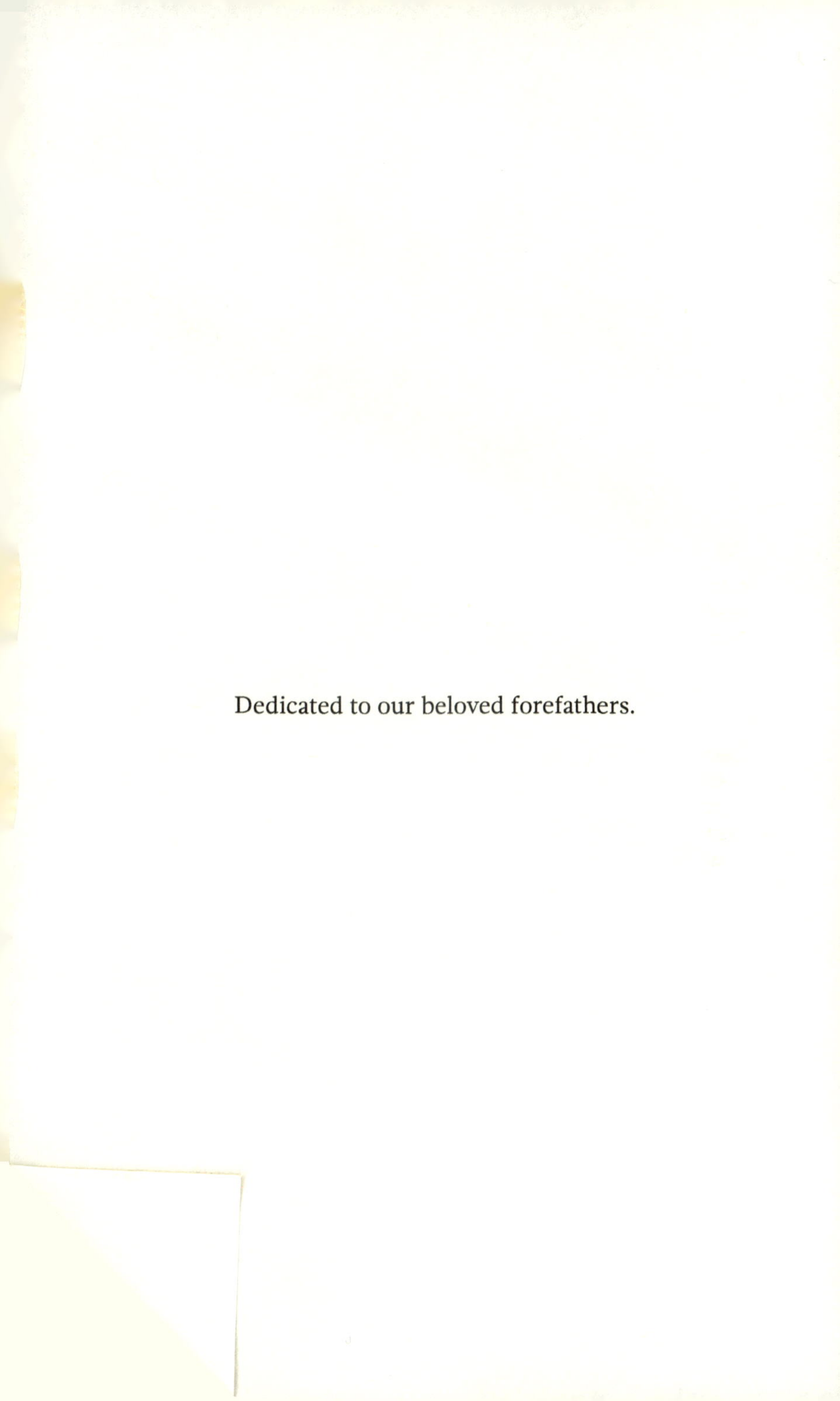

Dedicated to our beloved forefathers.

Contents

Foreword

This book deals with the role played by the Freedom Fighters in the Indian Independence Movement from Undivided Goalpara District of Assam.

Preface

This book deals with the role played by the Freedom Fighters in the Indian Independence Movement from Undivided Goalpara District of Assam. Hope the publication of this book will be useful. This book may not be free from errors and constructive criticisms are welcomed for the improvement of this book.

CHAPTER ONE

A Brief Introduction to the History of Assam

Assam was known as "Pragjyotishpura" or the city of eastern astrology and "Kamrupa" in ancient times, as evidenced from the great ephics- the Ramayana, the Mahabharata and other Indian scriptures, Puranas and poetical works. It was only after the advent of the Ahoms that, the state came to be known as "Assam". There are different opinions on the origin of the name. Some people are of the opinion that the word "Assam" is derived from the Sanskrit word "Asama" meaning uneven or unequal. And as the landscape of the state is mountainous and not plain so, this is the reason behind the name given to the state. While some others believe that Assam is only the anglicised version of "Asom", which is the name given to the state by the Ahoms after they conquered it. This version on the origin of the name sounds more realistic because of the fact that the state was being started to be called as "Assam" only after the conquest of Assam by the Ahoms. The 13th century witnessed the advent of the mighty Ahoms led by the legendary Chaolung Sukapha. After Sukapha's demise, many Ahom kings ruled over Assam.

It were the Britishers who pulled a curtain over the glorious 600 years rule of the Ahoms by signing the "Treaty of Yandaboo" with the Burmese on 24th February 1826. Since then, Assam came under the British rule. The British rule in Assam, however, saw some gloomy days and horrible nights, as the people of Assam united to revolt against the Britishers and an exciting saga of sacrifice and martyrdom began in Assam, which continued till India got independence. The freedom fighters of Assam, like Maniram Dewan, Kushal Konwar, Kanaklata Baruah, Mohiram Koch, Maniram Kachari, Mangal Kurmi, Bhogeshwari Phukanani, Dayal Chandra Panika, Lerela Boro and many others played a major role in the freedom struggle of Assam. It was only because of the courage, dedication, selflessness, patriotism and sacrifice of these and many other freedom fighters, that today, we are breathing in a free Assam and India.

CHAPTER TWO

ROLE PLAYED BY ASSAM IN THE INDIAN FREEDOM MOVEMENT

Assam played an important role in the history of country's freedom struggle. Gomdhar Konwar was the first Assamese to fight against the British. To regain the lost freedom of the motherland, he fought against the British along with Kandura Deka Phukan, Dharmadhar, Haranath and some other nobles. In 1828, the rebels attacked the British armoury at Sadiya. The British crushed this rebellion, but could not suppress the burning desire of freedom from the heart of the people of Assam. So started renewed preparation for another revolt. This time Piyali Barphukan took the lead. He was helped by Jiuram Dulia Barua, Benudhar Konwar, Rupchand Konwar, Deuram Dihingia, Boum Chingfau, Haranath and others. With this band of followers Piyali Barphukan decided to attack the British with an attempt to burn down the British camp at Rangpur.

The plan succeeded and the camp was destroyed. But the British captured Piyali Barphukan, Jiuram Barua and some others. Piyali and Jiuram were hanged and others deported for 14 years. During that time, another patriot named Gadadhar Gohain was planning an uprising with some native sepoys of the British army for and made an attempt to kill the British officials posted in upper Assam. But the British captured and imprisoned him before his plan could be materialised.

In 1857, when the Great Revolt shook the whole of the northern India, a brave and intelligent nobleman in Assam named Maniram Dewan took the lead to bring the revolt into this eastern corner. He went to Kolkata and with the help of another rebel named Madhu Mallik, he chalked out the plan for an uprising in Assam. From there he started sending letters to the last Ahom King Kandarpeswar Singha and his adviser Piyali Barua to keep them informed about the courses of the revolt. A loyal group consisting of both nobles and common people took part in Maniram's anti-British plot. Notable among them were Mayaram Nazir, Nilakanta Choladhara Phukan, Marangikhowa Gohain, Dutiram Barua, Bahadur Gaonburha, Farmud Ali, Trinayan, Kamala Barua and others. Some Hindusthani sepoys stationed at Sahabad also gave them support. According to the plan it was decided that the native soldiers would attack the British under the leadership of the Ahom King while Maniram advanced with arms and ammunitions from Kolkata. Unfortunately the attempt failed. A little lapse on the part of the rebels led the enemy to pre-empt the plan and immediately the British captured and imprisoned many of the rebels. Maniram was taken prisoner in Kolkata. The British also arrested Kandarpeswar Singha and imprisoned him. A great number of the patriots were deported to the

Andamans. On February 26, 1858, Maniram Dewan and Piyali Barua gave their lives at the gallows in Jorhat jail for 'high treason' against the British government.

Three years after, in 1861, a peasant uprising took place at Phulaguri in Nagaon district. The year 1894 also saw another peasant revolt at Patharughat in Darrang. In both of these events, the peasants raised bold protest against the exploitation and oppressive policy of the British Raj. The British ruthlessly subdued these uprisings and many peasants embraced martyrdom.

There was a brief lull, but the desire for freedom burned in the hearts of the Assamese people as a smouldering fire. The founding of the Indian National Congress in 1885 and the 'Swadeshi Andolan' after 'Partition of Bengal' in 1905 had great impacts on the patriotic people of Assam. With the appearance of Mahatma Gandhi in 1921 on the national scene, the freedom struggle in Assam also gained momentum along with the rest of India. Congress volunteers in thousands joined the 'Non-cooperation', 'Civil Disobedience' and other movements. The patriotic people of Assam jumped into both the unarmed movement led by Mahatma Gandhi and armed efforts of the revolutionaries. Chandranath Sarma, Nabin Chandra Bardoloi, Tarun Ram Phukan, Gopinath Bardoloi and others took the leadership of the freedom struggle in Assam.

On August 9, 1942, when Indian National Congress declared the 'Quit India' movement, it took an enormous shape in this part of the country. Able and efficient leaders like Gopinath Bardoloi, Bishnuram Medhi, Fakhruddin Ali Ahmed, Omeo Kumar Das, Jyotiprasad Agarwala, Hem Barua, Bijoy Chandra Bhagawati, Chandraprabha Saikiani, Puspalata Das led the movement organised by National Congress. The Socialist followers of Jayaprakash Narayan in Assam added immense momentum with their revolutionary activities. Though the 'Communist Party of India' (CPI) opposed the movement and rather supported the British on the pretext of their so called 'People's War', the members of a small communist group named 'Revolutionary Communist Party of India' (RCPI) engaged themselves in the patriotic struggle and revolutionary activities against the British war-efforts. The subversive activities indulged by the volunteers of 'Mrityu Bahini' of great socialist revolutionary leader Sankar Barua caused much anxieties for the British government. During 'Quit India' movement patriots like Kushal Konwar, Tilak Deka, Kanaklata Barua, Mukunda Kakati, Bhogeswari Phukanani, Mangal Kurmi, Maniram Kachari, Hemoram Pator, Gunabhi Bardoloi, Lerela Boro, Ratan Kachari, Lakhi Hazarika, Thagi Sut, Boloram Sut, Madan Barman, Rauta Boro, Nidhanu Rajbangshi and many others laid down their lives at the gallows, firings and other atrocities of the British Raj. Their heroic sacrifices inspired not only the people of this eastern tip but the whole nation. Bishnu Rabha, Haren Kalita, Haridas Deka, Khagen Barbora, Mathura Deka, Gobinda Kalita, Chatrasing Teron, Chintaharan Kalita, Nirendra Lahiri, Uma Sarma, Suresh Bhattacharya, Sarat Rabha, Mohanlal Mukherjee, Hena Ganguli of RCPI played significant role to intensify the revolutionary efforts in this region.

The flame of freedom now engulfed the whole subcontinent in such a magnitude that it became impossible for the foreign rulers to extinguish the fire. So, very soon the British had to quit India and on August 15, 1947 along with the rest of the nation, Assam was also illuminated with the light of long cherished freedom.

CHAPTER THREE

The Undivided Goalpara district is an erstwhile district of Assam, India, first constituted by the British rulers of Colonial Assam. Today the erstwhile Goalpara district is divided into Kokrajhar, Chirang, Bongaigaon, Dhubri, South Salmara (Mankachar) and Goalpara district. The name of the district Goalpara is said to have originally derived from 'Gwaltippika' meaning 'Guwali village' or the village of the milk men means (Yadav). The history of Goalpara goes back to several centuries. The district came under British rule in 1765. Before this, the area was under the control of the Koch dynasty. In 1826 the British accessed Assam and Goalpara was annexed to the North-East Frontier in 1874, along with the creation of district headquarters at Dhubri.

On 1 July 1983 two districts were split from Goalpara: Dhubri and Kokrajhar. On 29 September 1989 Bongaigaon district was created from parts of Goalpara and Kokrajhar. In 2003, Chirang District was created from parts of Kokrajhar and Bongaigaon districts. In 2016, South Salmara (Mankachar) District was created by bifurcating Dhubri district.

CHAPTER FOUR

Gurudev Kalicharan Brahma

The great social reformer Gurudev Kalicharan Brahma was born at Kazigaon village in the District of undivided Goalpra on 18th April 1860. Now his birth place is under Kokrajhar district of Bodoland Territorial Region. His father's Name was Kaulram Mech and Mother's was Randini Mech. Kaularam was a timber merchant and one of the rich persons of those days. From the childhood Kalicharan was a very intelligent, honest and thoughtful. He founded a new religion called "Brahma Dharma" in 1906 and he is reverentially called "Gurudev" or "Guru Brahma" by Bodo people of lower Assam along Brahmaputra river. He also became a great religious preacher of Brahma faith and brought over revolutionary changes in Bodo society by his continuous and sustained programme of reformation.

By the end of the 19th century and the early part of 20th century, the Bodo society was also politically degradation. The young Kalicharan Brahma could perceive the deplorable condition of the Bodos who were bogged down with social practices due to which the commitments despised them and he believed that Bodos are the original inhabitants of Assam. Later Kalicharan Brahma realized that Bodo society would have to be reformed. The Bodos were annoyed by other societies for their bad habits and ill practices. They were addicted to wine, rice bear and bad habits. Later Kalicharan Brahma achieved success in bringing changes among Bodo society in many fields by preaching his religious faith and principles and for which he was known as "Gurudev."

The basic ideology of "Brahma Dharma" preached by Gurudev Kalicharan Brahma is one "God" in the form of "Fire." "Fire" is "Brahma" and "Brahma" gives live to the entire earth and all its begins. "Brahma" is universal and endless. Where there is "Brahma", there can be found "Satya" or "Truth".

Satish Chandra Basumatary

Satish Chandra Basumatary was an Indian Bodo poet, dramatist, social worker and the second president of Bodo Sahitya Sabha. He is a pioneer people of Bibar era, the age of renaissance of Bodo literature. He is credited with helping established Bodo Brahma Dharma. He was also the editor of first Bodo magazine Bibar in 1924. He was honoured Mengnw Rwngwi Jwhwlao title after his death.

He was born on 16 November 1901 at Balukmari village in Dhubri district (present day Kokrajhar district) into a Bodo family. He was the son of Thandaram Basumatary andKhowlou Basumatary. He started schooling from Dhubri High School and later went to Cotton College, Guwahati. He died on 16 November 1974.

Rupnath Brahma

Rupnath Brahma was born on 15th June 1902 in a Bodo family at Owabari village near Kokrajhar town. Rupnath Brahma was an active worker of the 'Bodo Chatra Sanmilan' which was established by Gurudev Kalicharan Brahma in the year 1919.

Simon Commission was appointed in November 1927 by the British Conservative government under Stanley

Baldwin to report on the working of the Indian constitution established by the Government of India Act of 1919. The commission consisted of seven members- four Conservatives, two Labourites, and one Liberal - under the joint chairmanship of the distinguished Liberal lawyerSir John Simonand Clement Attlee, the future prime minister. Its composition met with a storm of criticism in India because Indians were excluded. The commission was boycotted by the Indian National Congress and most other Indian political parties. It, nevertheless, published a twovolume report, mainly the work of Simon.

Regarded as a classic state document, the report proposed provincial autonomy in India but rejected parliamentary responsibility at the centre. It accepted the idea of federalism and sought to retain direct contact between the British crown and the Indian states. Before its publication its conclusions had been outdated by the declaration of October 1929, which stated that dominion status was to be the goal of Indian constitutional development.

The coming of the Simon Commission in 1927 provided the necessary springboard for their switchover. The Simon Commission reached Assam in 1928 and remained functional in the state till January, 1929. The objective of this Commission was to inquire into the working of the system of Government, the growth of education, and development of representative institutions in British India and to report as to whether and to what extent; it was desirable to establish the principle of responsible Government. The Royal Notification served throughout the Indian Domain in March 6, 1928, called for memoranda, to be submitted to the Commission. The Boros too, submitted memoranda through different organizations of their community. Gurudev Kalicharan Brahma led the delegation team of the Goalpara District Community, while Jadav Khaklari submitted another memorandum as the Secretary of the Assam Kachari Juba Sanmelan, on behalf of the entire Boro community of Assam.The memoranda urged the Government to grant a separate electorate for the Boro-Kachari community, both in the Assembly and local board elections; to provide compulsory free primary education to the students of this community. The memoranda also appealed the Government not to transfer Assam to Bengal province and recommended for a single chamber ministry for Assam. The memoranda submitted by the Boro-Kachari organizations however did not receive due response from the Government. Intellectuals, who have gone through the original report of the Commission sense foul-play by an Assamese member, who was entrusted with the responsibility of receiving the memoranda from the organizations.However, the memorandum submitted by the Provincial Government redressed Boro grievances to some extent.

He was serious about his education and therefore refused to join the Quit India Movement of 1921 during his college days, for he realized at a very young age that he had to siphon the knowledge acquired, to help his brother Bodos to emancipate. Although he was born in a privileged Timber Merchant's family and was an Advocate (first law graduate from Bodo society) by profession, he quit practising as he did not enjoy the ways and mores of the profession and could not taste success like some of his contemporaries in the then Dhubri Court, who took full advantage of lack of education and simplicity of the poor Bodo people.

He decided to follow the path of Kalicharan Brahma of working towards the development of Bodos and the other Tribal groups as well. Therefore, he came into close contact with him and jointly took up several social welfare activities for the Bodos and other backward communities.

The Government of India Act 1935 sowed the seeds of Political aspirations among Bodos and other backward Tribals in Assam as it provided for the reservation of six seats in the Provincial Assembly for the Plains Tribes. Rupnath was not only qualified but he wanted to work towards the uplift of the depressed classes. Hence, he was elected as one of the representatives, in the 1937 General Election. Later he won from the Sidli Constituency on the ticket of The Tribal League. This election was a historic moment for the Tribal League because as many as five representatives from the Tribal League had been elected to the Provincial Legislature and they could float their concerns and put up the demands of the Tribal people on the floor of the Assembly.

Rupnath Brahma in his speech in the Assam Legislative Assembly Proceedings (ALAP) of 5th August 1937 had raised the issue of preserving the 'Line System'' and he cited the example of erstwhile Goalpara "Many Tribal people in Goalpara have been compelled to leave their homes and settle elsewhere". Therefore, he and his colleagues from The Tribal League could gauge the treacherous intention of the Muslim League related to the 'Line System'. Hence the Tribal League backed the Indian National Congress (INC) and played a pertinent role by coming down heavily on the Muslim League and subsequently the government fell on 13th September 1938, which in turn played a decisive factor in the win of INC led by Gopinath Bardoloi on 19th September 1938.

Subsequently, Rupnath was rewarded for his effort and was given the portfolio of the Minister of Forest and Registration as a nominee of the Tribal League. When Rupnath Brahma was the president of All Assam Plains Tribal League he had sent a memorandum to His Excellency the Viceroy stating that the proposed grouping of Assam with Bengal has naturally created a sense of great disapproval and resentment and that the Tribal people of Assam are unanimously against the inclusion of Assam with Bengal.

Rupnath also lamented; that authorities had sidelined the issue of education of Backward Tribal people of the region. In his Assam Legislative Assembly Proceedings (ALAP) speech on 18th February 1938; he said that he was disappointed with the fact that the government had not earmarked provision for the Plain Tribal people in that year's Budget even though Tribals were the most Backward in the region. He further said; "If there is no definite move from the government for the education of these people, then I think all nation-building projects will be left far behind in Assam". Rupnath (who had studied in a Bengali medium school) had realized that as a result of the Treaty of Yandaboo; till 1872 Bengali was the medium of instruction and although; Assamese was reintroduced but in many schools of lower Assam Bengali was still the medium of instruction; therefore Rupnath Brahma along with Kalicharan Brahma and Sarat Goswami made relentless efforts to introduce Assamese as a medium of instruction in erstwhile Goalpara instead of the prevailing Bengali medium at that time.

Rupnath had the opportunity to serve the backward and downtrodden tribals when he became a member of the Advisory Committee of the Minority Sub-Committee or

Bardoloi sub-committee formed on 27th February 1947. As a member of these committees, he obtained some facilities from the Central Government that would serve the interest of the Tribals. As a member of the Assam Tribal and Excluded Areas Sub-Committee, he rendered yeoman's service to the Sub-Committee. The present Sixth Schedule was added to the Constitution of India on the recommendation of this Sub-Committee.

The Tribal Leaguewas formed in1933 under the leadership of Rupnath Brahma and Rabi Chandra Kachari. In 1937, the Muslim League moved a resolution for the abolition of the Line system. Members of the Tribal League, Rabi Chandra Kachari, and Rupnath Brahma opposed the resolution and it was eventually withdrawn. The Tribal League had to fight with the Muslim League under the leadership of Maulavi Saiyid Muhammad Saadulla in Assam Legislative Assembly from 1937 to 1946. Then Tribal League had joined hands with Indian national congress under the leadership of Gopinath Bodoloi after independence.

Jogendra Kumar Basumatary

Jogendra Kumar Basumatary (19 May 1920- 28 March 2010) was an Indian writer and social worker from Bodo community. He was elected as a president of Bodo Sahitya Sabha held in 1983. He received the first U.N. Brahma Soldier of Humanity Award in 2004.

He was born on 19 May 1920 at Gosaigaon village under Manikpur circlein Goalpara district (present day Kokrajhar district) of Assam. He was the son of Arindra Basumatary and Gilashri Basumatary. He breathed his last on 28 March 2010.

Jogendra Kumar Basumatary was not only a writer and social worker but also a freedom fighter. Police arrested him twice for participating in the freedom struggle. During Quit India Movement, he was arrested and jailed for 6 moths at Guwahati jail.

After independence, he was honoured with Tamrapatra by the Central Goverment and granted him pension in 1973. The State Goverment honoured also him in 1993 by giving him literary pension for his valuable contribution to the Bodo literature. The Upendranath Brahma Trust (UNBT) also honoured him with its first UN Brahma Soldier of Humanity Award for his immense contribution in all fields during 2004.

CHAPTER FIVE

Finally, Assam became a part of the Indian Union only after a tug-of-war between the Congress and Tribal Leagueversus Muslim League.Mohammad Ali Jinnah made strong claims for the state's inclusion in Pakistan but tenacious opposition from the Congress leadership in the state with Mahatma Gandhi's direct support saved Assam from joining Pakistan.The Assam Congress's determined opposition ensured that the arrangement did not take off. The Cabinet Mission may have sought to preserve the unity of India, but it compromised with the Muslim League on the inclusion of Assam, a Hindu majority province, in Pakistan.

In February 1946, Pethic Lawrence, the then secretary of state for India, circulated a note on the viability of Pakistan. In the note, he mentioned that Assam, due to economic, defence and financial considerations, was to form part of East Pakistan. The Assamese were aghast and felt this was a clever British ploy to keep their commercial interests intact. The Cabinet Mission sought to camouflage its real intention by keeping the grouping clause vague and created an impression that they were not serious about exerting pressure on Assam in consonance with the Muslim League's demand.

On May 16 1946, the Cabinet Mission recommended that Assam and Bengal be tagged together to frame the provisional constitutions for the provinces.The Mission laid stress on provincial autonomy and viewed that every province be constituted on a linguistic and cultural basis. The recommendation came by despite the appearance of Assam Premier Gopinath Bardoloi before the Mission.Bardoloi said, "Assamhad always been a separate state with a distinctive identity and must be allowed to remain in India under a provincial status."

However, Saadullah, leader of the Muslim League in the Assam assembly, suggested that the province could be attached to Bengal. This helped Lawrence in forming a belief that Assam had such a close connection with Bengal that its separation from Bengal was impossible.

The Assam Pradesh Congress Committee was taken aback to find the Cabinet Mission toeing Saadullah's line by tagging Assam along with Bengal.The APCC felt that small provinces like Assam would be forced to accept a dispensation which would largely be determined by the majority of another province.

But the Congress leadership seemed to treat Assam's case on a low key. It perhaps apprehended that taking up the issue at that stage might result in confusion and a stalemate of the larger priority of India's freedom.

It was thanks to Gandhi's support that the Congress Working Committee adopted a more responsible attitude to the Assam problem.

It was only because of the contributions made by Gopinath Bordoloi, Rupnath Brahma and other tribal leaders that Assam was prevented from becoming a part of Pakistan.

References

Bukumar.V. (2013). Social Exclusion and Ethnicity in North-East India. The NEHU Journal. Vol. XI, I-2, pp-19-35.

Col Ved.P (2007). Encyclopedia of North-East India. Atlantic Publishers and Distributors Pvt.Ltd; New Delhi. Vol.5.

Rao,V.V., Hazarika.N (1983). A Century of Government and Politics in North-East India. S.Chand and Company Pvt.Ltd; New Delhi. Vol. I.